White Trash

By
Laraine Shape

CCC PUBLICATIONS

Published by

CCC Publications
1111 Rancho Conejo Blvd.
Suites 411 & 412
Newbury Park, CA 91320

Manufactured in the United States of America

Cover/Interior production by Oasis Graphics

ISBN: 0-57644-026-5

If your local U.S. bookstore is out of stock, copies of this
book may be obtained by mailing check or money order for
$5.95 per book (plus $2.50 to cover postage and handling)
to: CCC Publications, 1111 Rancho Conejo Blvd.,
Suites 411 & 412, Newbury Park, CA 91320

Pre-publication Edition - 7/96

DEDICATION

This homemade "work-of-trash" is dedicated to my family; to the people of Waterville, Ohio; to my co-workers (including those on extended "leaves of absence" in various state and federal institutions) and to people in general...most of whom I truly adore.

<< >>

And to Hub and June, wherever you are today, thank you for blessing me with a sense of humor.

YOU KNOW YOU'RE
WHITE TRASH
IF . . .

You've ever scraped your elbows trying to get something out of a dumpster

Your kids use
Cheeze Whiz®
in place of
toothpaste

You clean fish on your ironing board

* * *

Your favorite color is shiny

You wish you
could bend your
head down as
far as your
dog can

You fix slower-
than-dog-shit
traffic lights with
a 12 gauge
shotgun

YOU KNOW YOU'RE
WHITE TRASH
IF . . .

You know where
to get
government
cheese

YOU KNOW YOU'RE WHITE TRASH IF . . .

Your attorney can be reached at 1-800-WIP-LASH

7

Your kids are the
source of school
head lice
epidemics

YOU KNOW YOU'RE
WHITE TRASH
IF . . .

Your kids end up
on milk cartons
before you
notice they're
missing

Your wife thinks
her thighs look
thinner in
Spandex®

YOU KNOW YOU'RE WHITE TRASH IF . . .

You keep your shed more secure than your house

11

Your husband's
idea of an
extended orgasm
is holding back
until he gets his
zipper down

You've seen
someone spray
their telephone
with Lysol® after
you used it

Your kids give
new meaning to
the term 'nose
mining'

You put
Kool-Aid® in
baby bottles

You wish those nosy, pencil-pushin' retards at the Division of Insurance Fraud would leave you the hell alone

YOU KNOW YOU'RE
WHITE TRASH
IF . . .

You live in
Toledo, Ohio
because you
want to

Your job skills
include being
handy with a
cattle prod and
knowing how to
roll back an
odometer

You've ever told
your wife that
Jean-Claude
Van Damme
is a Homo

YOU KNOW YOU'RE WHITE TRASH IF . . .

You keep spare Ferris wheel parts in your shed

Your wife asks
about layaway at
flea markets

Your girlfriend
breaks her ankle
bracelets on
your rear view
mirror

Your idea of good luck is finding arm rest towels to match leopard skin slip covers

Your dad had a
real knack for
finding things at
the dump that
were "too
damned good"
to be thrown
away

YOU KNOW YOU'RE
WHITE TRASH
IF . . .

Your wife poses
for the BEFORE
pictures in
miracle weight
loss ads

You've ever threatened to kill one of the neighbor kids for messing with your tackle box

Your wife's
favorite wedding
present was a
pair of welding
goggles

You think a pap
smear is what
your daddy
wipes on his
jeans after a
healthy sneeze

You know which
end of the
chicken a
possum prefers
to eat first

The sight of a
Slim Jim® makes
your wife's
mouth water

You know how mountain oysters taste, or for that matter, you know what they are

You think
Samsonite® is
someone you
read about in
the Bible

You'd rather
watch Cops than
Seinfeld

You bought a
metal detector
after your kids
found a quarter
buried in the
sofa cushions

Your mom and
dad shared
everything –
including a
set of teeth

Your refrigerator
has a coat of
auto primer on it

Your boss has to
check with the
probation
department
before firming up
reservations for
company picnics

Your contest entry on "How to Avoid the Repo Man" won you a new set of jumper cables

Your mother once told a State Trooper she'd take a breathalyzer when her butt learned how to chew bubblegum

You pay extra lot rent for the privilege of being within walking distance to the dumpster

YOU KNOW YOU'RE WHITE TRASH IF . . .

You crochet things for toasters and toilet paper

You smoke
fish in
your trunk

Your bridal
registry can be
found at Ace®
Hardware or
Dollar General®

YOU KNOW YOU'RE
WHITE TRASH
IF . . .

You grew up
believing a
woman with
no teeth
was gifted

Your idea of foreplay is telling your wife she better be in bed by the time you count to 4

45

Your wife's idea
of redecorating
is moving her
Avon® bottles
around

YOU KNOW YOU'RE WHITE TRASH IF . . .

Your boss invited you to go hunting when he found out you could make duck calls with your armpit

YOU KNOW YOU'RE
WHITE TRASH
IF . . .

One of your
relatives went
bankrupt after
winning the
lottery

Your husband remembers your bra size since it's the same as his IQ

You get discount
coupons from
the abortion
clinic

**YOU KNOW YOU'RE
WHITE TRASH
IF . . .**

Your husband
uses engine
degreaser in
place of
shampoo

51

YOU KNOW YOU'RE
WHITE TRASH
IF . . .

You buy
teeth through
the mail

52

You have to cut the feet off your panty hose so you can get them over your ankles

Your sister runs a
dating service on
her CB called
Trucker Tail

Your car seat covers used to be a chenille bedspread

**YOU KNOW YOU'RE
WHITE TRASH
IF . . .**

You've ever been
tempted to make
a night crawler
chip dip

Your local
laundromat
doubles as
your day
care center

You figure you're entitled to use 7-Eleven as your business address since you use the pay phone and restroom there

Your first training bra came from GoodWill and had cups the size of basketball hoops

You've tried to
get credit
with your
sweepstakes
finalist
notifications

Your dad always
thought that
having more than
one toothbrush
in the house was
a waste of
money

**YOU KNOW YOU'RE
WHITE TRASH
IF . . .**

Your kids take
empty beer bottles
to school for
Show-and-Tell

Your boss keeps
a bail bondsman
on the payroll –
just in case

You've ever had to fish one of your wife's favorite shoes out of the septic tank

You think a mammogram is that funny little picture they're putting on credit cards now

Your kids think
Hamburger
Helper® is one
of the major
food groups

You've ever
taken a six pack
to a graveside
service

YOU KNOW YOU'RE
WHITE TRASH
IF . . .

Your wife says she'd dust more often if you bought her a leaf blower.

You went ahead and ordered that blackhead remover since it came with a free potato peeler

Your husband
caught the sofa
on fire trying to
light farts

You've ever asked the police if your kids get to keep what they stole

Your wife fixes
the dents in her
car with a STOP
sign and spot
welder

YOU KNOW YOU'RE
WHITE TRASH
IF . . .

Your kids supply the
neighborhood with
WILL WORK FOR
FOOD signs

73

You've ever been
assaulted with a
toilet seat

* * *

You know how
to fish with a
baseball bat

Your kids have to call a 1-900 phone sex number if they need to reach you at work

You store an emergency six-pack in the toilet tank

✳ ✳ ✳

Your dashboard doubles as a religious shrine

You take your kids sledding with a garbage can lid, a rope and a Trans Am

YOU KNOW YOU'RE WHITE TRASH IF . . .

You respond to "Earn Big $$ Money At Home" advertising

You lost interest
in your wife after
she lost 250
pounds

* * *

You know how
to disassemble a
merry-go-round

You have
cockroaches big
enough to ride

* * *

You've never had
to file a tax
return

Your outdoor
Christmas lights
cost more
than your
trailer did

Your dentist can't clean your teeth without gagging

✳ ✳ ✳

You took and passed the Civil Service Exam

You know
anything about
barnyard science
or animal
husbandry

Your wife wants
to convert the
camper into a
mobile dog
grooming salon

YOU KNOW YOU'RE
WHITE TRASH
IF . . .

You refuse to live
in a trailer park
that has speed
bumps

Your husband's
idea of a wet
dream is a
free case of Old
Milwaukee®

YOU KNOW YOU'RE WHITE TRASH IF . . .

You use the garden hose to clean your living room carpet

✳ ✳ ✳

You keep bait in your refrigerator

The only thing
your wife uses a
steam iron on is
grilled cheese
sandwiches

You've ever tried to buy Girl Scout cookies with food stamps

Your wife had
a hysterectomy
so she could
grow a better
mustache than
you

Your husband's
one and only
sexual fantasy
involves a
Roto-Rooter®

YOU KNOW YOU'RE
WHITE TRASH
IF . . .

You wrote a Dear
Abby letter when
your rabbit had
baby kittens

The image
of Jesus
mysteriously
appears on
the side of your
mobile home

Your
grandmother
wears a T-shirt
that says
JUST BLOW ME

You've ever
mooned a gun
control rally

＊＊＊

The smell of bait
makes you
homesick

Your sister takes steroids for PMS

✳ ✳ ✳

You met your girlfriend at a construction site

You carry
your lunch in
something that
can be fixed
with Bondo®

The smell of
diesel fuel
makes you miss
your wife

YOU KNOW YOU'RE
WHITE TRASH
IF . . .

Your toupee
looks like it was
made in the
blender with cat
hair and
wallpaper paste

99

You've ever spent an unemployment check on Harley parts and lotto tickets

You trim your
husband's back
hair with a weed
whacker

YOU KNOW YOU'RE
WHITE TRASH
IF . . .

You've ever sent
your husband
to the store
for a box of
Carp-Helper

You own
anything with
fringe on it

✳ ✳ ✳

Your wife wears
panty hose
under shorts

**YOU KNOW YOU'RE
WHITE TRASH
IF . . .**

Your husband calls his Wet Vac® "Precious"

✳ ✳ ✳

You have a relative who collects bicycle seats

Your teeth
and gums are
featured in a
periodontal
brochure

Your mail order business is featured in the FBI's training manual

Your appearance on Oprah gave viewers a better understanding of justifiable homicide and mountain law

Your local beauty shop doubles as a dog grooming salon

YOU KNOW YOU'RE WHITE TRASH IF . . .

You have the VFW Post and Psychic Hot Line on speed dial

YOU KNOW YOU'RE
WHITE TRASH
IF . . .

Your husband
proposed to
you at a
Dunkin' Donuts®
counter

110

**YOU KNOW YOU'RE
WHITE TRASH
IF . . .**

The high school
football team
came to your
baby shower

* * *

Your mom knows
how to make
cotton candy

YOU KNOW YOU'RE WHITE TRASH IF . . .

You've ever gone to an Amway® meeting on purpose

You think being
double-jointed
entitles you
to additional
welfare benefits

YOU KNOW YOU'RE
WHITE TRASH
IF . . .

You get
concerned when
the price of
scrap metal
drops

YOU KNOW YOU'RE WHITE TRASH IF . . .

Your husband's idea of a weakness is the government's idea of a felony offense

YOU KNOW YOU'RE WHITE TRASH IF . . .

Your son Bud is named after what was on tap the night he was born

YOU KNOW YOU'RE
WHITE TRASH
IF . . .

You started your
own business
with a bucket,
a flash light and a
frog gig

117

YOU KNOW YOU'RE WHITE TRASH IF . . .

You've ever moved your family to Florida with a homemade trailer, no job prospects and less than $20 in your pocket

You've never
seen an
encyclopedia
salesman, Fed-Ex
truck or Realtor
in your
neighborhood

YOU KNOW YOU'RE
WHITE TRASH
IF . . .

You have trouble
getting over
speed bumps
when your wife
is in the car

Your husband's
idea of getting
lucky is passing
a vehicle
emissions test

**YOU KNOW YOU'RE
WHITE TRASH
IF . . .**

Your family
portrait looks
like a science
project gone
awry

You once spent an entire afternoon explaining to police what you were doing in the sub-division wearing only a hunting cap and a pair of binoculars

You've ever
broken a set of
knuckles or toes
on a vending
machine

YOU KNOW YOU'RE
WHITE TRASH
IF . . .

You can gauge
wind direction with
your wife's facial
hair

✳ ✳ ✳

You've ever tried to
buy real estate with
no money down

YOU KNOW YOU'RE WHITE TRASH IF . . .

Your home town has the word Beaver or Lick in it

* * *

Your boss lets you trim your toe nails at work

126

YOU KNOW YOU'RE
WHITE TRASH
IF . . .

You've ever
worked for the
IRS on purpose

Your wife pawned her wedding ring to raise dog show entry fees

The words
"rehab", "rodeo"
or "roadside"
show up on your
job applications

YOU KNOW YOU'RE
WHITE TRASH
IF . . .

Your family was
the subject of a
genetic research
project

Your husband owns a book called "How To Earn a Fortune In The Lawnmower Engine Repair Business"

You've ever made it your business to find out how long the eviction process takes

You have
something on
your property
that people pay
to see

You've ever put
a 911 operator
on hold while
you grabbed
a cold one

You've ever
taken a job you
found in the
"seasonal"
section of the
want ads

**YOU KNOW YOU'RE
WHITE TRASH
IF . . .**

You wrote for
information on
how to erase
bad credit
instantly

136

YOU KNOW YOU'RE
WHITE TRASH
IF . . .

Your kids make
Slurpees with
yellow snow

YOU KNOW YOU'RE
WHITE TRASH
IF . . .

Your attorney
makes house-
trailer calls

Your wife uses
Preparation-H®
on her
thighs

You've ever
dreamed of
being on a TV
game show

You know
what head
lice shampoo
smells like

Your last sighting
was featured in
the National
Enquirer

YOU KNOW YOU'RE
WHITE TRASH
IF . . .

Your life
has been
one long
bad hair day

You started
carrying two sets
of ID after
you were born
again

You can't apply
for jobs that
require owning
your own
tools

You mend
your clothes
with a
stapler

YOU KNOW YOU'RE
WHITE TRASH
IF . . .

Your dish
towels double
as shop rags

YOU KNOW YOU'RE WHITE TRASH IF . . .

You wore a sleeveless wedding gown so people could see your tattoos

YOU KNOW YOU'RE WHITE TRASH IF . . .

Your wife knows how to run a backhoe

YOU KNOW YOU'RE WHITE TRASH IF . . .

You own a nightgown that lights up

150

You've ever
appeared on TV
with a talking
dog

You've never been
given keys to
anything at work

YOU KNOW YOU'RE WHITE TRASH IF . . .

You know, or have ever worked with the author of this book

153

TITLES BY CCC PUBLICATIONS

Retail $4.99
"?" book
POSITIVELY PREGNANT
WHY MEN ARE CLUELESS
CAN SEX IMPROVE YOUR GOLF?
THE COMPLETE BOOGER BOOK
FLYING FUNNIES
MARITAL BLISS & OXYMORONS
THE VERY VERY SEXY ADULT DOT-TO-DOT BOOK
THE DEFINITIVE FART BOOK
THE COMPLETE WIMP'S GUIDE TO SEX
THE CAT OWNER'S SHAPE UP MANUAL
PMS CRAZED: TOUCH ME AND I'LL KILL YOU!
RETIRED: LET THE GAMES BEGIN
THE OFFICE FROM HELL
FOOD & SEX
FITNESS FANATICS
YOUNGER MEN ARE BETTER THAN RETIN-A
BUT OSSIFER, IT'S NOT MY FAULT

Retail $4.95
YOU KNOW YOU'RE AN OLD FART WHEN...
1001 WAYS TO PROCRASTINATE
HORMONES FROM HELL II
SHARING THE ROAD WITH IDIOTS
THE GREATEST ANSWERING MACHINE MESSAGES OF ALL
  TIME
WHAT DO WE DO NOW?? (A Guide For New Parents)
HOW TO TALK YOU WAY OUT OF A TRAFFIC TICKET
THE BOTTOM HALF (How To Spot Incompetent Professionals)
LIFE'S MOST EMBARRASSING MOMENTS
HOW TO ENTERTAIN PEOPLE YOU HATE
YOUR GUIDE TO CORPORATE SURVIVAL
THE SUPERIOR PERSON'S GUIDE TO EVERYDAY IRRITATIONS
GIFTING RIGHT

Retail $5.95
LOVE DAT CAT
CRINKLED 'N' WRINKLED
SIGNS YOU'RE A GOLF ADDICT
SMART COMEBACKS FOR STUPID QUESTIONS
YIKES! IT'S ANOTHER BIRTHDAY
SEX IS A GAME
SEX AND YOUR STARS
SIGNS YOUR SEX LIFE IS DEAD
40 AND HOLDING YOUR OWN

50 AND HOLDING YOUR OWN
MALE BASHING: WOMEN'S FAVORITE PASTIME
THINGS YOU CAN DO WITH A USELESS MAN
<u>MORE</u> THINGS YOU CAN DO WITH A USELESS MAN
THE WORLD'S GREATEST PUT-DOWN LINES
LITTLE INSTRUCTION BOOK OF THE RICH & FAMOUS
WELCOME TO YOUR MIDLIFE CRISIS
GETTING EVEN WITH THE ANSWERING MACHINE
ARE YOU A SPORTS NUT?
MEN ARE PIGS / WOMEN ARE BITCHES
ARE WE DYSFUNCTIONAL YET?
TECHNOLOGY BYTES!
50 WAYS TO HUSTLE YOUR FRIENDS ($5.99)
HORMONES FROM HELL
HUSBANDS FROM HELL
KILLER BRAS & Other Hazards Of The 50's
IT'S BETTER TO BE OVER THE HILL THAN UNDER IT
HOW TO REALLY PARTY!!!
WORK SUCKS!
THE PEOPLE WATCHER'S FIELD GUIDE
THE UNOFFICIAL WOMEN'S DIVORCE GUIDE
THE ABSOLUTE LAST CHANCE DIET BOOK
FOR MEN ONLY (How To Survive Marriage)
THE UGLY TRUTH ABOUT MEN
NEVER A DULL CARD
RED HOT MONOGAMY (In Just 60 Seconds A Day) ($6.95)
HOW TO SURVIVE A JEWISH MOTHER ($6.95)
WHY MEN DON'T HAVE A CLUE ($7.99)
LADIES, START YOUR ENGINES! ($7.99)

Retail $3.95
NO HANG-UPS
NO HANG-UPS II
NO HANG-UPS III
HOW TO SUCCEED IN SINGLES BARS
HOW TO GET EVEN WITH YOUR EXES
TOTALLY OUTRAGEOUS BUMPER-SNICKERS ($2.95)

NO HANG-UPS – CASSETTES Retail $4.98

Vol. I:	GENERAL MESSAGES (Female)
Vol. I:	GENERAL MESSAGES (Male)
Vol. II:	BUSINESS MESSAGES (Female)
Vol. II:	BUSINESS MESSAGES (Male)
Vol. III:	'R' RATED MESSAGES (Female)
Vol. III:	'R' RATED MESSAGES (Male)
Vol. IV:	SOUND EFFECTS ONLY
Vol. V:	CELEBRI-TEASE

FOR ADDITIONAL COPIES
SEND THIS COUPON TO

CCC PUBLICATIONS
1111 Rancho Conejo Blvd.
Suite 411 & 412
Newbury Park, CA 91320

Please send me _____ copies of The Book Of
White Trash Single copies $5.95 ea. plus
$2.50 per order to cover postage and handling
(Check or Money Order).

NAME

ADDRESS

CITY   STATE   Zip

WANTED!
Vendors & Retailers

Cash in on the fun! Sell The Book of White Trash from
your booth, shop, grab stand or trunk. Fast and easy way
to raise money for bail, Trans Am parts, attorney fees,
tattoos, lap dances, dog show entry fees or lotto tickets!

For information on volume discounts write to:

CCC PUBLICATIONS
1111 Rancho Conejo Blvd.
Suite 411 & 412
Newbury Park, CA 91320